Odysseus and the Cyclops

Retold by Rod Theodorou
Illustrated by Barry Wilkinson
Series Editor: Rosalind Kerven

Introduction

The story of Odysseus and the Cyclops is part of a long poem called 'The Odyssey'.
'The Odyssey' was written by an Ancient Greek poet called Homer.
This is one of the earliest pieces of Greek writing.

Map of Ancient Greece

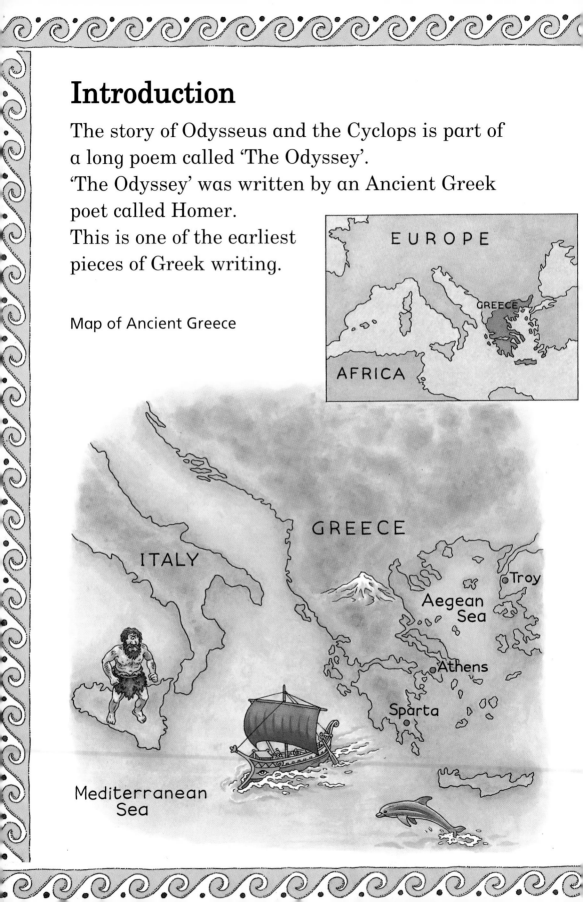

A Cunning Greek

Homer's poem 'The Odyssey' is about a cunning Greek called Odysseus.
Odysseus and many other Greeks fought a long war with the people of Troy. 'The Odyssey' is the story of Odysseus' journey back from Troy to his home.

We beat the Trojans because of a trick Odysseus played on them. Can you find out what the trick was?

On his journey Odysseus met with gods, monsters and magic. It was always Odysseus' cunning which kept him alive.

The Ancient Greeks liked to paint pictures of their myths and legends. This Greek vase shows Odysseus blinding the Cyclops. ▶

Long ago
a boat sailed across the lonely sea.
It was taking Odysseus and his
men home after a long war.
But now they were lost.
"Look!" Odysseus shouted, "Land!"
It was an island.

The boat landed on the strange island.
The men looked up at the towering hills, dotted
with huge caves.
"I fear," said Odysseus, "that we have
landed on the Island of the Cyclopes."

"Cyclopes!" said Odysseus' men, "Let's go!"

"No," said Odysseus.

"I want to see what they're like.

Perhaps we can give them presents and make friends."

Odysseus chose twelve of his best men.

They packed some food and wine-skins and

climbed up to the nearest cave.

They entered the giant cave.
They could see sheep and some huge
logs, but no Cyclopes.
They lit a fire and waited.
Suddenly they heard footsteps.
Something was coming . . .something very big.

In walked a man as big as a shaggy mountain.
In the middle of his forehead was one
shiny black eye like a giant grape.
It was a Cyclops!

"I can see you!"

The Cyclops rolled a huge stone across
the entrance to the cave.
Then he saw the Greeks.
"Strangers!" said the Cyclops.
"What are you doing in my cave?
Don't try to run away."

9

"We are shipwrecked sailors," said Odysseus.
"A storm blew us on to your island.
Please let us rest here and find food.
The gods say everyone should be kind to strangers."

10

The Cyclops laughed.
His laugh was as loud as thunder.
"I am stronger than the gods!
Tell me," he said, licking his lips.
"Where are the rest of your men?"
Odysseus did not trust the Cyclops.
He said, "We are the only men left alive."

Without saying another word the Cyclops grabbed
two men and ate them for his supper.
It was horrible to watch.
Odysseus' men cried out in terror.

The Greeks ran to hide, but there was
no escape from the cave.
Odysseus had an idea.
He picked up some wine-skins and went to
talk to the Cyclops.
"Cyclops," said Odysseus, "if I give you
this wine as a gift, will you let us go?"

The Cyclops grabbed the wine and
drank it all in three gulps.
"That was good!" he said.
 "What is your name?"
"My name is . . . Nobody," said Odysseus.
"Well, Nobody," said the Cyclops, "I will
give you a gift. I will eat you last!"

14

Then the Cyclops fell down into a deep drunken sleep.
Odysseus' men picked up their swords.
"Let's kill him," they said.
Odysseus stopped them.
"If we kill him we will be trapped forever," he said.
"None of us could move that giant stone."

Then Odysseus had an idea.

"Bring that log over here," he said.

The men carried the log to Odysseus.

Odysseus sharpened the end of the log to
make a giant spear.

They put the end of the spear into the fire.

Then they carried the spear over to the Cyclops.

His eye was shut.

They pointed the spear at his eye.

(You can guess what they did next.)

Aaaaaaaargh!

The Cyclops bellowed.
The walls shook.
Rocks fell down from above.
"Help me!   Help me!" cried the Cyclops.

18

The screams of the Cyclops carried for miles.
Outside the cave other Cyclopes came out of
their caves to see what was happening.
"What's the matter?" they said.
"Has someone hurt you?"

"Nobody has hurt me," cried the Cyclops.
"Nobody has tricked me.
It's Nobody! It's Nobody!"

"Nobody?" said the other Cyclopes.
"If nobody has hurt you we'll all go back to bed."
The other Cyclopes left.

Odysseus and his men were still trapped.
The Cyclops rolled back the great stone to
let his sheep out to feed.
He sat at the entrance to stop the men going out.
"How are we going to escape?" they said.
Odysseus had another idea.

He tied the Cyclops' sheep together, in threes.
Each man clung under three sheep.
The sheep went out of the cave.
The Cyclops patted each sheep on the
back, but he didn't find the men.

23

Odysseus and his men ran back to their ship.
They took the Cyclops' sheep with
them and rowed out to sea.
Odysseus shouted back to the Cyclops,
"Next time, Cyclops, listen well to the
laws of the gods!"